What's on your Mind?

Discover the Power of Biblical Thinking

D1316333

John Goetsch

First published in 2010 by Striving Together Publications, a ministry of Lancaster Baptist Church, Lancaster, CA 93535. Striving Together Publications is committed to providing tried, trusted, and proven books that will further equip local churches to carry out the Great Commission. Your comments and suggestions are valued.

Striving Together Publications
4020 E. Lancaster Blvd.
Lancaster, CA 93535
800.201.7748

Cover design by Andrew Jones
Layout by Craig Parker
Edited by Cary Schmidt and Maggie Ruhl
Special thanks to our proofreaders.

ISBN 978-1-59894-104-3

Printed in the United States of America

Table of Contents

The Created Mind

Key Verses

ISAIAH 55:8–9

8 *For my thoughts are not your thoughts, neither are your ways my ways, saith the* LORD.

9 *For as the heavens are higher than the earth, so are my ways higher than your ways, and my thoughts than your thoughts.*

Lesson Summary

The fascinating and complex human mind points to the evidence of its Creator. This lesson reveals how a designed creation under divine control has the capacity to make choices that lead to a successful, God-fulfilled life.

Lesson Aim

To fundamentally prove that God is the designer of the mind, and His creation is designed to glorify Him.

Introduction

_____

_____

_____

I. Our Minds Are _____ Creations

A. *Created by the _____*

B. *Calling for our _____*
PSALM 139:13–17

13 For thou hast possessed my reins: thou hast covered me in my mother's womb.

14 I will praise thee; for I am fearfully and wonderfully made: marvellous are thy works; and that my soul knoweth right well.

15 My substance was not hid from thee, when I was made in secret, and curiously wrought in the lowest parts of the earth.

16 Thine eyes did see my substance, yet being unperfect; and in thy book all my members were written, which in continuance were fashioned, when as yet there was none of them.

17 How precious also are thy thoughts unto me, O God! how great is the sum of them!

II. Our Minds Are under a _____ Control

A. *A _____ mind*

B. *A _____ mind*

III. Our Minds Can Make _____ Choices

A. A choice to _____

B. A chance to _____

GENESIS 3:1–6

1   Now the serpent was more subtil than any beast of the field which the LORD God had made. And he said unto the woman, Yea, hath God said, Ye shall not eat of every tree of the garden?

2   And the woman said unto the serpent, We may eat of the fruit of the trees of the garden:

3   But of the fruit of the tree which is in the midst of the garden, God hath said, Ye shall not eat of it, neither shall ye touch it, lest ye die.

4   And the serpent said unto the woman, Ye shall not surely die:

5   For God doth know that in the day ye eat thereof, then your eyes shall be opened, and ye shall be as gods, knowing good and evil.

6   And when the woman saw that the tree was good for food, and that it was pleasant to the eyes, and a tree to be desired to make one wise, she took of the fruit thereof, and did eat, and gave also unto her husband with her; and he did eat.

GENESIS 39:7–10

7   And it came to pass after these things, that his master's wife cast her eyes upon Joseph; and she said, Lie with me.

8   But he refused, and said unto his master's wife, Behold, my master wotteth not what is with me in

the house, and he hath committed all that he hath to my hand;

9   There is none greater in this house than I; neither hath he kept back any thing from me but thee, because thou art his wife: how then can I do this great wickedness, and sin against God?

10   And it came to pass, as she spake to Joseph day by day, that he hearkened not unto her, to lie by her, or to be with her.

Conclusion

_____

_____

_____

Study Questions

1. Who is the creator of your mind? See John 1:3.

2. What is the most intricate of all creations? See Psalm 139:13–17.

3. In a split second of time between temptation and response, our minds have the ability to make a choice. Compare and contrast the following stories in the Bible: Eve and the serpent (Genesis 3:1–6) and Joseph (Genesis 39:7–10). How were their responses to temptation different? Were their temptations similar?

4. God has placed boundaries on your mind—your knowledge and understanding. Do you find yourself trusting your logic—your limited mind—instead of God's omniscience? List five areas in your life in which you need to trust God.

5. Write out the wise counsel David gave to his son in 1 Chronicles 28:9.

6. Ken Collier once said, "Only two choices on the shelf: pleasing God or pleasing self." What five choices can you make this week that will please and glorify God?

7. Proverbs 1:10 shows you when to make a particular choice, and it even tells you the right choice to make. Write out this verse.

8. Spend time every day this week asking the Creator to *"Let the words of my mouth, and the meditation of my heart, be acceptable in thy sight, O LORD, my strength and my redeemer"* (Psalm 19:14).

Memory Verses

ISAIAH 55:8–9

8 For my thoughts are not your thoughts, neither are your ways my ways, saith the LORD.
9 For as the heavens are higher than the earth, so are my ways higher than your ways, and my thoughts than your thoughts.

The Changed Mind

Key Verses

LAMENTATIONS 3:22–23

22 It is of the LORD's mercies that we are not consumed, because his compassions fail not.

23 They are new every morning: great is thy faithfulness.

Lesson Summary

Paul challenges the thinking of those who were gathered on Mars' Hill. While they were being open-minded to the pluralistic thinking of their day, Paul admonished them to "change their minds"—stop looking to lifeless idols and start looking to the living God. This lesson penetrates right to the heart of the matter and focuses on establishing a solid relationship with God.

Lesson Aim

To place ourselves in a relationship with a living God, for when we do, we'll quickly see the need for a changed mind.

Introduction

_____

_____

_____

I. He Presents a _____ God

A. The _____ of lifeless gods

B. The _____ of a living God
DANIEL 6:17–22, 24–27

17 And a stone was brought, and laid upon the mouth of the den; and the king sealed it with his own signet, and with the signet of his lords; that the purpose might not be changed concerning Daniel.

18 Then the king went to his palace, and passed the night fasting: neither were instruments of musick brought before him: and his sleep went from him.

19 Then the king arose very early in the morning, and went in haste unto the den of lions.

20 And when he came to the den, he cried with a lamentable voice unto Daniel: and the king spake and said to Daniel, O Daniel, servant of the living God, is thy God, whom thou servest continually, able to deliver thee from the lions?

21 Then said Daniel unto the king, O king, live for ever.

22 My God hath sent his angel, and hath shut the lions' mouths, that they have not hurt me: forasmuch as before him innocency was found in me; and also before thee, O king, have I done no hurt.

24 And the king commanded, and they brought those men which had accused Daniel, and they cast them into the den of lions, them, their children, and their wives; and the lions had the mastery of them, and brake all their bones in pieces or ever they came at the bottom of the den.

25 Then king Darius wrote unto all people, nations, and languages, that dwell in all the earth; Peace be multiplied unto you.

26 I make a decree, That in every dominion of my kingdom men tremble and fear before the God of Daniel: for he is the living God, and stedfast for ever, and his kingdom that which shall not be destroyed, and his dominion shall be even unto the end.

27 He delivereth and rescueth, and he worketh signs and wonders in heaven and in earth, who hath delivered Daniel from the power of the lions.

II. He Presents a _____ God

A. A God of _____

B. A God of _____

III. He Presents a _____ God

A. A _____ for repentance

B. A _____ to revolutionize

Conclusion

_____

_____

_____

Study Questions

1. Write out the words that describe God in Psalm 103:8.

2. What does God command of every man in Acts 17:30?

3. How does the story of Daniel in the lions' den prove the fact that a living God does exist? See Daniel 6:18–27.

4. Ezekiel 18:30 says, "...*Repent, and turn yourselves from all your transgressions; so iniquity shall not be your ruin.*" Write down the sins with which you struggle most. Review this list and repent of your sins to your Heavenly Father. Then, explain how you plan to turn from these transgressions the next time Satan tries to tempt you with them.

5. Write out the command of repentance in Acts 8:22.

6. What gods do you trust to deliver you? Do you find yourself relying on money, power, success, or relationships to fulfill your needs in life more than you do the God of Heaven? How can 1 Thessalonians 1:9 challenge you to put your trust in the right place?

7. When answering to a lawful God, the problem isn't the deed of sin; the problem lies with the doer of the deed. Read Ezekiel 18:30–31 and summarize the truths found in these verses as they relate to repentance of sin.

8. God is patient and longsuffering (Lamentations 3:22–23). Throughout your daily routines this week, strive to be more like your Heavenly Father in this area, and ask Him to help you be patient with your relationships, inconveniences, deadlines, and even yourself as you grow more in Him. Read Lamentations 3:22–23 and be encouraged.

Memory Verses

LAMENTATIONS 3:22–23

22 *It is of the LORD's mercies that we are not consumed, because his compassions fail not.*
23 *They are new every morning: great is thy faithfulness.*

The Conscientious Mind

Key Verses

ECCLESIASTES 12:13–14

13 *Let us hear the conclusion of the whole matter: Fear God, and keep his commandments: for this is the whole duty of man.*

14 *For God shall bring every work into judgment, with every secret thing, whether it be good, or whether it be evil.*

Lesson Summary

This lesson teaches about the response of those on Mars' Hill to Paul's insistent and convicting plea—they didn't listen! Many people have seared consciences when it comes to hearing the truth of God's Word, and because of their deadened ears to God's plea, they mock, rebel, and turn from repentance. This lesson centers on the study of a seared conscience and the detrimental effects it can have.

Lesson Aim

To help students understand that we only have one life, and this life is the only chance we get to prepare to meet God.

Introduction

_____

_____

_____

I. God's Word Declares an Inescapable

_____

A. *Our sure* _____

B. *Our soon* _____

II. God's Word Declares an Incredible

_____

A. *No one is* _____.

B. *No one can* _____.

III. God's Word Declares an Impenitent

_____

A. *God has* _____ *clearly.*

B. *Man has* _____ *consciously.*

IV. God's Word Declares an Impending

_____

A. A revealing _____

B. A restricted _____

Conclusion

_____

_____

_____

PROVERBS 1:22–33

22 How long, ye simple ones, will ye love simplicity? and the scorners delight in their scorning, and fools hate knowledge?

23 Turn you at my reproof: behold, I will pour out my spirit unto you, I will make known my words unto you.

24 Because I have called, and ye refused; I have stretched out my hand, and no man regarded;

25 But ye have set at nought all my counsel, and would none of my reproof:

26 I also will laugh at your calamity; I will mock when your fear cometh;

27 When your fear cometh as desolation, and your destruction cometh as a whirlwind; when distress and anguish cometh upon you.

28 Then shall they call upon me, but I will not answer; they shall seek me early, but they shall not find me:

29 For that they hated knowledge, and did not choose the fear of the LORD:

30 They would none of my counsel: they despised all my reproof.

31 Therefore shall they eat of the fruit of their own way, and be filled with their own devices.

32 For the turning away of the simple shall slay them, and the prosperity of fools shall destroy them.

33 But whoso hearkeneth unto me shall dwell safely, and shall be quiet from fear of evil.

Study Questions

1. When a hot iron is placed on the flank of an animal, it hurts! But once the flesh has been "seared" with the hot iron, it is deadened to all feeling. Consider this illustration when you read 1 Timothy 4:1–2. What did Paul mean when he said, "...*having their conscience seared with a hot iron*"?

2. How does the Bible describe someone with a seared conscience? See Proverbs 29:1 and Ephesians 4:19.

3. Many times, the problem with someone who has a seared conscience is that he does not want to give up his sin. John 3:19 says, "...*men loved darkness rather than light, because their deeds were evil.*" God's Word has the ability to transform you, renew you, and change a seared conscience. Do you have any sin that you are holding onto right now to which your conscience has become deadened over time?

4. Conviction from the Holy Spirit can be uncomfortable, but when God's Word speaks, listen. The worst thing that can happen to you is when that still, small voice goes silent. Be honest with yourself and write briefly what the Holy Spirit has been convicting you about recently. If you can't think of anything, spend time in prayer asking God's Spirit to convict you of your sins.

5. Daniel Webster once said, "The greatest thought that can occupy a man's mind is his accountability to God." Write out the following verses that correspond with Daniel Webster's statement: Acts 17:31, Hebrews 9:27, and Amos 4:12.

6. As Paul pleads with those on Mars' Hill to change their minds and turn to Christ, how do they respond? (See Acts 17:32)

7. No matter who you are or what you have done, whether saved or lost, you will meet God. Referencing 1 John 2:28, describe in your own words what instruction is given to you before this meeting will take place.

8. What point was the most convicting to you in this study and why?

Memory Verses

ECCLESIASTES 12:13–14

13 *Let us hear the conclusion of the whole matter: Fear God, and keep his commandments: for this is the whole duty of man.*
14 *For God shall bring every work into judgment, with every secret thing, whether it be good, or whether it be evil.*

The Captured Mind

Key Verse

2 CORINTHIANS 10:5

5 Casting down imaginations, and every high thing that exalteth itself against the knowledge of God, and bringing into captivity every thought to the obedience of Christ;

Lesson Summary

While some hardened to the message of God from Paul, others heeded. Acts 17 ends on an encouraging note! Just like the few on Mars' Hill who believed God's truth, God wants to capture our minds with truth as well. This lesson focuses on challenging every student to bring "*into captivity every thought to the obedience of Christ*" (2 Corinthians 10:5).

Lesson Aim

To encourage and challenge every student to be spiritually minded—living out every routine, schedule, or situation with the mind of Christ.

Introduction

_____

_____

_____

I. The Captured Mind Begins with an _____

A. A desire to _____

B. A diligence to _____

II. The Captured Mind Proceeds with an _____

A. A _____ of deference

B. A _____ with disobedience

III. The Captured Mind Culminates in an _____

A. The process of a _____ mind

B. The pertinence of a _____ mind

Conclusion

_____

_____

_____

Study Questions

1.   The captured mind begins with what?

2.   Since we cannot wash our minds out with soap, how can we cleanse our minds? See John 15:3.

3.   When right thinking takes place, right living will follow. Referencing Joshua 1:8, summarize the steps to right living and take special note of the first step.

4.   Think back to the last spiritual truth you were taught and then read James 4:17. Have you obeyed that spiritual truth? What does the Bible say about knowing to do good and not doing it?

5.   The blessing of God rests on those who not only hear, but who also obey. Write out what the Scriptures say about obedience in James 1:22–25.

6.   In Acts 17:34, the two converts, Dionysius and Damaris, opened their minds to truth in such a way that they had an impact on others. How can you specifically follow God's truth in such a way that you will have an impact on those around you?

7. Because the way you think affects the way you live, wrong thinking of the past needs to be replaced by right thinking. Make a list of two or three thoughts that you struggle with the most (e.g., faithless thoughts, envious thoughts, jealous thoughts, etc.), and list two or three verses that will help you overcome them.

8. An assignment for this week: Every time you hear God's Word expounded upon (whether through preaching or teaching), pray beforehand that God will open your heart and mind to the truth He wants you to hear. Be encouraged as God will answer this prayer and reveal to you the truths and principles He wants applied to your life.

Memory Verse

2 CORINTHIANS 10:5

5 *Casting down imaginations, and every high thing that exalteth itself against the knowledge of God, and bringing into captivity every thought to the obedience of Christ;*

The Complacent Mind

Key Verse

MATTHEW 5:6

6 Blessed are they which do hunger and thirst after righteousness: for they shall be filled.

Lesson Summary

Laziness and idleness—these two qualities are far too prevalent in this generation. Students have a hard time doing their homework because they just don't feel like it. Adults are no longer as well-read because they prefer a TV sitcom over a good book. Our generation has become experts at being ignorant; however, the Apostle Paul personally demonstrates how to avoid having a lazy and idle mind. This lesson focuses on how Paul challenged his mind, searched the Scriptures, gave attendance to reading, and developed a sound mind.

Lesson Aim

To develop a sound mind by searching the Scriptures, listening to preaching, and developing good reading habits.

Introduction

_____

_____

_____

I. The Challenge of a _____ Mind

   A. Give attendance to _____.

   B. Give adherence to _____.

II. The Challenge of a _____ Mind

   A. The stirring of _____

   B. The seduction of _____

III. The Challenge of a _____ Mind

   A. The _____ of a sound mind

   B. The _____ of a sound mind

Conclusion

_____

_____

_____

Study Questions

1. First Timothy 4:13 says to give attendance to what three things?

2. What two evils did the people commit in Jeremiah 2:13?

3. Describe your Bible reading. Is it beneficial, consistent, thorough, and applicable to your daily life? After referring to John 5:39 and 2 Timothy 2:15, how can you enhance your time spent in the Bible?

4. In your own words, explain how this statement is true: "A lazy person tempts the devil to tempt him."

5. God's Word comforts the distressed and distresses the comfortable. We need the exhortation of God's Word to stir us up to truth. Write the following verses regarding biblical exhortation: Hebrews 3:12–13.

6. According to Isaiah 26:3, our minds must be stayed upon whom in order to get perfect peace?

7.   List the last three books you have read outside of the Bible, and answer the following questions. Were these books edifying? Christ-honoring? Helpful? Or, were they time-wasters? Ineffective? Dishonoring to Christ?

8.   Be encouraged as you read Matthew 11:28–30. Write out a prayer telling God about the heavy burdens you carry. Choose to lay these at His feet so that He may give you rest.

Memory Verse
MATTHEW 5:6

6   Blessed are they which do hunger and thirst after righteousness: for they shall be filled.

The Careless Mind

Key Verse

JOSHUA 1:8

8 This book of the law shall not depart out of thy mouth; but thou shalt meditate therein day and night, that thou mayest observe to do according to all that is written therein: for then thou shalt make thy way prosperous, and then thou shalt have good success.

Lesson Summary

Paul went to a lot of trouble to mentor Timothy in the truth of God's Word. The responsibility was now Timothy's. Instead of acting careless with the truths he had been taught, Timothy determined to cultivate truth in his heart so that he could mature spiritually. D.L. Moody once said, "I never saw a useful Christian who was not a student of the Bible." Like Timothy, we can learn to avoid carelessness in our minds by becoming useful Christians—students of God's Word.

Lesson Aim

To discipline our thoughts in the right direction so that we can live the right result.

Introduction

_____

_____

_____

I.   A _____ of Truth

A. A _____ *for cultivation*

B. A _____ *for cultivation*
2 PETER 3:14–18

14 Wherefore, beloved, seeing that ye look for such things, be diligent that ye may be found of him in peace, without spot, and blameless.

15 And account that the longsuffering of our Lord is salvation; even as our beloved brother Paul also according to the wisdom given unto him hath written unto you;

16 As also in all his epistles, speaking in them of these things; in which are some things hard to be understood, which they that are unlearned and unstable wrest, as they do also the other scriptures, unto their own destruction.

17 Ye therefore, beloved, seeing ye know these things before, beware lest ye also, being led away with the error of the wicked, fall from your own stedfastness.

18 But grow in grace, and in the knowledge of our Lord and Saviour Jesus Christ. To him be glory both now and for ever. Amen.

II. A _____ of Truth

  A. _____ the Word of God.

  B. _____ to the Word of God.

III. A _____ with Truth

  A. A _____ thought

  B. A _____ truth

Conclusion

_____

_____

_____

Study Questions

1. Philippians 4:8 tells us to think on which things?

2. Reading and memorizing God's Word early in the day will allow you to "think" on it throughout the day. List two Scriptures that support this truth.

3. D.L. Moody said, "I never saw a useful Christian who was not a student of the Bible." Do you consider yourself a student of the Bible? Explain your answer.

4. You are to discipline your thoughts in the right direction so that you can live the right way. Psalm 119:59 says, *"I thought on my ways, and turned my feet unto thy testimonies."* Think on your ways, and determine whether you need to turn back to God's Word. What changes do you need to make?

5. The prophets of the Old Testament understood the need to cultivate the heart. Write out their exhortations in Jeremiah 4:3 and Hosea 10:12.

6. In your own words, describe what it means to delight in the Law of the Lord (Psalm 1:2).

7. What command is given in 2 Peter 3:18, and what steps can you take toward fulfilling it?

8. Using Psalm 4:4 as a guide, spend some quiet time with the Lord, commune with Him, and ask Him to help you cultivate truth in your heart.

Memory Verse

JOSHUA 1:8

8 *This book of the law shall not depart out of thy mouth; but thou shalt meditate therein day and night, that thou mayest observe to do according to all that is written therein: for then thou shalt make thy way prosperous, and then thou shalt have good success.*

The Contaminated Mind

Key Verse

PROVERBS 12:5

5   *The thoughts of the righteous are right: but the counsels of the wicked are deceit.*

Lesson Summary

Unlike light switches, our minds do not turn on and off instantly. Although that would be convenient, it's just not possible. Instead, we have to work on turning our minds off and keeping them closed to wrong influences. Paul was aware of this, and in 1 Timothy 4:16, he warns Timothy to take heed and be careful lest his mind be contaminated. We too can slip into the role of Paul's pupil and learn how to guard our minds from contamination.

Lesson Aim

To guard our minds from wrong influences by keeping our lives pure before God.

Introduction

_____

_____

_____

I. A Closed Brain-Door Will Keep Your _____ Clean

A. The _____ of a clear _____

B. The _____ of a clean _____

II. A Closed Brain-Door Will Keep Your _____ Centered

A. The content of _____

B. The concern of _____

PSALM 119:97–106

97 _O how love I thy law! it is my meditation all the day._

98 _Thou through thy commandments hast made me wiser than mine enemies: for they are ever with me._

99 _I have more understanding than all my teachers: for thy testimonies are my meditation._

100 _I understand more than the ancients, because I keep thy precepts._

101 I have refrained my feet from every evil way, that I might keep thy word.

102 I have not departed from thy judgments: for thou hast taught me.

103 How sweet are thy words unto my taste! yea, sweeter than honey to my mouth!

104 Through thy precepts I get understanding: therefore I hate every false way.

105 Thy word is a lamp unto my feet, and a light unto my path.

106 I have sworn, and I will perform it, that I will keep thy righteous judgments.

III. A Closed Brain-Door Will Keep Your _____ Clear

A. *A pure* _____

B. *A pleased* _____

Conclusion

_____

_____

_____

Study Questions

1. What are the three benefits of having a closed brain-door?

2. God has chosen that His Word should flow through you, and He requires that it flow through a clean conduit. What steps can you take in your life to make yourself a clean conduit for God's truth?

3. According to Jeremiah 17:9, can we trust the thoughts in our hearts?

4. When God's Word is valuable to you, your values will be right. Refer to Psalm 119:97–106 and explain how this concept directed the psalmist's life.

5. All of us have said things that we regret. Perhaps in frustration you have said, "Why did I say that?" But way before we stop our tongue, we must stop our thoughts. Write out Matthew 12:33–35 to help you think before you speak.

6. Because we can't trust ourselves to think right, we must saturate ourselves with the truth that God has given to us. List three ways you can saturate yourself with the truth of God's Word.

7. There is an old computer saying that says, "Garbage in—Garbage out." As you consider the thoughts you struggle with most, ask yourself, "What 'Garbage in' is filtering into my heart and mind causing me to think these thoughts?" Next, read Matthew 12:33–35, and write out the truths found in these verses.

8. When you are thinking right, with the Holy Spirit's help the right words will come when you need them. Assignment for this week: Look for a chance to tell someone about the Lord, and allow God to show you that He will give you the right words to say if you first commit your thoughts to Him.

Memory Verse

PROVERBS 12:5

5   *The thoughts of the righteous are right: but the counsels of the wicked are deceit.*

The Closed Mind

Key Verse

1 PETER 5:8

8   Be sober, be vigilant; because your adversary the devil, as a roaring lion, walketh about, seeking whom he may devour:

Lesson Summary

In 1 Timothy 4, Paul is very specific about why it is so important to keep a closed mind. With approximately ten thousand thoughts going through our brain waves every day, it is easy for the wrong things to slip in. This lesson focuses on why having a closed mind is essential to living a Christ-pleasing life.

Lesson Aim

To close our minds to unrighteous thoughts as they come through various diversions, demands, and deceptions.

Introduction

_____

_____

_____

I. A Closed Mind Guards against _____ Deception

A. The _____ of Satan

B. The _____ of Satan

1 JOHN 4:1–6

1   Beloved, believe not every spirit, but try the spirits whether they are of God: because many false prophets are gone out into the world.

2   Hereby know ye the Spirit of God: Every spirit that confesseth that Jesus Christ is come in the flesh is of God:

3   And every spirit that confesseth not that Jesus Christ is come in the flesh is not of God: and this is that spirit of antichrist, whereof ye have heard that it should come; and even now already is it in the world.

4   Ye are of God, little children, and have overcome them: because greater is he that is in you, than he that is in the world.

5   They are of the world: therefore speak they of the world, and the world heareth them.

6   We are of God: he that knoweth God heareth us; he that is not of God heareth not us. Hereby know we the spirit of truth, and the spirit of error.

II. A Closed Mind Guards against _____ Demands

A. *The tendency to _____ biblical principles*

B. *The time to _____ biblical principles*

III. A Closed Mind Guards against _____ Diversions

A. *Guarding our minds from _____ diversions*

B. *Growing our minds for _____ destination*

IV. A Closed Mind Guards against _____ Diligence

A. *God's _____ program*

B. *God's _____ proclaimed*

V. A Closed Mind Guards against _____ Departure

A. *Your establishment of _____*

B. *Your effect on the* _____

Conclusion

_____

_____

_____

Study Questions

1. We must guard our minds against heretical deception. How can we do this according to 1 John 4:1–6?

2. Good things can keep us from the best things. First Corinthians 6:12 says, *"All things are lawful unto me, but all things are not expedient: all things are lawful for me, but I will not be brought under the power of any."* As you review your priorities in life, do you see any areas where something good takes priority over that which is best?

3. Look at your to-do list this week. Make a list of items from your to-do list that will last for eternity. What items can you add to next week's to-do list that will have more of an impact on eternity?

4. We must guard our minds against any teaching that makes demands not found in God's Word. In light of this principle, write out Proverbs 30:5–6.

5. Read 1 Timothy 4:1. What will happen in the latter times according to this verse?

6. Relive the story of Naaman in the Old Testament. He had his own way of searching out a cure for leprosy, and when he was confronted with God's way of healing, he at first refused. Do you have any preconceived beliefs about God or His Word that may keep you from obeying what the Bible truly says (2 Kings 5)?

7. It is amazing how diligent and disciplined we can be in the areas of little importance. You may make time to watch the big game, watch the news, go to work, each lunch, work out, etc., but how diligent are you in godliness?

8. Prayerfully, you will meet people in Heaven who are there because of your prayers, giving, or testimony. However, meditate on this sobering question, "Will there be anyone in Hell because of you?"

Memory Verse

1 PETER 5:8

8 *Be sober, be vigilant; because your adversary the devil, as a roaring lion, walketh about, seeking whom he may devour:*

The Censored Mind

Key Verse

ROMANS 12:2

2   *And be not conformed to this world: but be ye transformed by the renewing of your mind, that ye may prove what is that good, and acceptable, and perfect, will of God.*

Lesson Summary

In our modern world of technology, we undeniably need the tool of censorship. We need to put restrictions on the television, the internet, other forms of media, and the list can go on. We also need to censor something far more valuable and important—our minds! Through Spirit-filled men, the Word of God, and a hatred for sin, God shows us how to censor our minds in Ephesians 4.

Lesson Aim

To be *"wise unto that which is good, and simple concerning evil"* (Romans 16:19).

Introduction

_____

_____

_____

I. Through the _____ of Called _____

A. The _____ helps build people.

B. The _____ has been prepared.

II. Through the _____ of Christ-like

_____

EPHESIANS 4:12–16

12 For the perfecting of the saints, for the work of the ministry, for the edifying of the body of Christ:

13 Till we all come in the unity of the faith, and of the knowledge of the Son of God, unto a perfect man, unto the measure of the stature of the fulness of Christ:

14 That we henceforth be no more children, tossed to and fro, and carried about with every wind of doctrine, by the sleight of men, and cunning craftiness, whereby they lie in wait to deceive;

15 But speaking the truth in love, may grow up into him in all things, which is the head, even Christ:

16 From whom the whole body fitly joined together and compacted by that which every joint supplieth, according to the effectual working in the measure of every part,

maketh increase of the body unto the edifying of itself in love.

A. A _____ *service*

Salvation   **Sanctification**   Glorification

├──┤

B. A _____ *stick*

III. Through the _____ over Corrupted _____

A. *The presence of* _____

B. *The power of* _____

Conclusion

_____

_____

_____

Study Questions

1. We are to protect our minds with the help of the authority God has placed over us. According to Hebrews 13:7 and 17, how are we to respond to our authority?

2. According to Titus 1:3, through what does God manifest His Word?

3. To have minds that are Christ-like and mature, we must be a student of the gifts God has given to us. The Apostle Paul answers the question, "Why did God give us human gifts?" Read Ephesians 4:12–16 and summarize his answer.

4. In a very general sense, there are three stages in God's plan for our lives. The first stage is salvation, which takes place the moment you put your faith and trust in Jesus Christ. List and describe the other two stages.

5. Write out Ephesians 4:17–18—a passage of Scripture which admonishes us not to walk in vanity or corrupt morality.

6. A continual process of censoring our minds will make us wise concerning good and simple concerning evil. (Romans 16:19). In your own words, why do you think it is best to be simple concerning evil?

7. According to Romans 12:2, how can we be transformed?

8. If God has changed your *destiny*, then let Him change your *demeanor*, so that others can see Christ in you. What changes can you make this week to clearly show others that Christ lives in you?

Memory Verse

ROMANS 12:2

2   *And be not conformed to this world: but be ye transformed by the renewing of your mind, that ye may prove what is that good, and acceptable, and perfect, will of God.*

The Clean Mind

Key Verse

2 CORINTHIANS 5:17

17 *Therefore if any man be in Christ, he is a new creature: old things are passed away; behold, all things are become new.*

Lesson Summary

When we get saved, we become new creatures in Christ. Although this is an exciting time, we must realize that we do not become perfect creatures in Christ. The struggle with sin and temptation still exists. Ephesians 4:19–20 gives us the process of how we allow sin into our minds even after salvation, and this lesson focuses on what we can do to keep our minds clean from that sin.

Lesson Aim

To help students understand the value and priority of having clean and pure minds before God, and to help them focus on the biblical way of keeping sin out of their minds.

Introduction

_____

_____

_____

I. An _____ Conscience

A. A _____ *mind*

B. A _____ *message*

II. An _____ Corruption

A. *The _____ of wrong* _____

B. *The _____ of woeful* _____

III. An _____ Continuation

A. *Sin _____ continually.*

B. *Sin _____ consciously.*

IV. An _____ Clamoring

A. *The _____ of sin*

B. The _____ of sin

V. An _____ Communication

A. The warning _____

B. The warning _____

Conclusion

_____

_____

_____

Study Questions

1. When we open the door of our minds to the thought of sin, we are asking for big problems. The following Scriptures contain warnings about sin. Look up these verses and write a sentence summarizing each verse: Romans 13:14, Ephesians 4:27, and Proverbs 1:10.

2. In the battle of trying to keep our minds clean from sin, the devil tries to create an appetite for sin. What do the following verses say about having an appetite for sin: Proverbs 15:14 and Job 15:16?

3. Through the process of closing our minds to God, the Holy Spirit tries to warn us. Are you ignoring God's warnings today? Does Isaiah 65:12 describe your response to God's warnings? Explain your answer.

4. Describe the last time you sensed God's Holy Spirit leading you. What was He asking, and how did you respond?

5. Sin begins with a thought and grows into an action. Write out James 1:14–15—the Bible's clear process of sin.

6. When you read Romans 1:32, you will find that the appetite for sin only grows. Meaning, we can get to the point where we enjoy the sin that we once detested. Think back to the time when you first became a Christian. God was now living inside of you, and you were determined to live your best for Him. Are there any sinful habits you have let back into your life since you became a Christian?

7. According to 2 Corinthians 5:17, what is to be "passed away"?

8. Ephesians 4:20 says, *"But ye have not so learned Christ."* Paul warned that allowing sin into a clean mind is not of Christ. Determine this week to learn Christ—learn His way of turning from temptation, His way of rebuking sin, and His way of following God's leading.

Memory Verse

2 CORINTHIANS 5:17

17 Therefore if any man be in Christ, he is a new creature: old things are passed away; behold, all things are become new.

The Conformed Mind

Key Verse

2 CORINTHIANS 3:5

5   Not that we are sufficient of ourselves to think any thing as of ourselves; but our sufficiency is of God;

Lesson Summary

This lesson introduces an error-proof formula for every Christian who desires to have the mind of Christ. It encourages each Christian to please God in the sincerest way by conforming his thoughts, desires, reactions, opinions, and beliefs in such a way that emulates Christ. These three practical steps of conforming our minds are intended to motivate us to godliness and holiness.

Lesson Aim

To establish a desire in the heart of each Christian to conform his mind to the mind of Christ.

Introduction

_____

_____

_____

I. _____ of Sinful _____

A. The _____ of sinful thought patterns

B. The _____ of sinful thought patterns

II. _____ with Spirit-Filled _____

A. The _____ of the Spirit

B. The _____ of self

III. _____ with Scriptural Precepts

A. *Putting* _____ *is equivalent to* _____.
PSALM 1:1–2
1   Blessed is the man that walketh not in the counsel
of the ungodly, nor standeth in the way of sinners, nor
sitteth in the seat of the scornful.
2   But his delight is in the law of the LORD; and in
his law doth he meditate day and night.

EPHESIANS 4:28

28 Let him that stole steal no more: but rather let him labour, working with his hands the thing which is good, that he may have to give to him that needeth.

ROMANS 12:9–21

9 Let love be without dissimulation. Abhor that which is evil; cleave to that which is good.

10 Be kindly affectioned one to another with brotherly love; in honour preferring one another;

11 Not slothful in business; fervent in spirit; serving the Lord;

12 Rejoicing in hope; patient in tribulation; continuing instant in prayer;

13 Distributing to the necessity of saints; given to hospitality.

14 Bless them which persecute you: bless, and curse not.

15 Rejoice with them that do rejoice, and weep with them that weep.

16 Be of the same mind one toward another. Mind not high things, but condescend to men of low estate. Be not wise in your own conceits.

17 Recompense to no man evil for evil. Provide things honest in the sight of all men.

18 If it be possible, as much as lieth in you, live peaceably with all men.

19 Dearly beloved, avenge not yourselves, but rather give place unto wrath: for it is written, Vengeance is mine; I will repay, saith the Lord.

20 Therefore if thine enemy hunger, feed him; if he thirst, give him drink: for in so doing thou shalt heap coals of fire on his head.

21 *Be not overcome of evil, but overcome evil with good.*

B. Putting _____ is equivalent to _____.

Conclusion

_____

_____

_____

Study Questions

1. What are we to do with our wickedness according to Acts 8:22?

2. List three or four sinful thought patterns that could threaten your life's direction.

3. What analogy does the Scripture use in Ephesians 5:18?

4. The replacement theory—putting off the sinful nature and putting on a Spirit-filled life—is found throughout the Bible. God emphasizes "replacement" in several places throughout Scripture. Read the following Scriptures and summarize each replacement that was made: Psalm 1:1–2, Ephesians 4:28, and Romans 12:9–21.

5. The old must be replaced by that which is new. Write out Colossians 3:8–10.

6. We cannot conform our minds to the mind of Christ in our own power. Read 2 Corinthians 3:5 and explain where we can get strength sufficient enough for this task.

7. List the three practical steps given in this lesson which lead to a mind conformed to Christ.

8. "Unless we have within us that which is above us, we will soon give in to the pressures around us." How can this quote help you live out your regular schedule this week?

Memory Verse

2 Corinthians 3:5
5   *Not that we are sufficient of ourselves to think any thing as of ourselves; but our sufficiency is of God;*

The Christ-Like Mind

Key Verses

PHILIPPIANS 2:5–8

5 *Let this mind be in you, which was also in Christ Jesus:*

6 *Who, being in the form of God, thought it not robbery to be equal with God:*

7 *But made himself of no reputation, and took upon him the form of a servant, and was made in the likeness of men:*

8 *And being found in fashion as a man, he humbled himself, and became obedient unto death, even the death of the cross.*

Lesson Summary

A recent trend started with the question, "What would Jesus do?" but this study encourages students to ask, "What would Jesus think?" In the last lesson, we learned to conform our minds to Christ's, and in this lesson, we are going to learn how to use our conformed minds by developing the characteristics of a Christ-like mind.

Lesson Aim

To challenge each student to get their thoughts out of the way by developing the mind of Christ.

Introduction

_____

_____

_____

I. A Mind of _____

A. *The ladder of no _____*

B. *The lesson of narcissistic _____*

II. A Mind of _____

A. *The great _____*

B. *A genuine _____*

III. A Mind of _____

A. *The mind of Christ is to _____.*

B. *The mind of Christ is by the _____.*

Conclusion

_____

_____

_____

Study Questions

1. God wants us to have selfless minds. However, when you read Romans 1:25, does this verse describe your Christianity? Explain your answer.

2. The greatest goal we could have for our lives is to be a servant. We are to have Christ's mind, and His mind is to serve. How can you serve God's people this week? In what ways can you serve more this week than you did last week?

3. Are you willing to do anything that God asks you to do? Is there anything that you are unwilling to do?

4. P. T. Forsyth said, "The purpose in life is not to find your freedom, but your Master." Give five reasons that show how you are living a life that is directed to becoming more like your Master. (Example: (1) I memorize Scripture to have the mind of Christ.)

5. When we get "our thoughts" out of the way, we can then develop the mind of Christ. Write out Ephesians 4:20–21.

6. According to Romans 15:3, not one single day of Jesus' eternal existence was ever lived for Himself. What did He live for according to John 8:29?

7. After reading 2 Timothy 3:2, what does *"For men shall be lovers of their own selves"* mean?

8. How will you choose to live the rest of your life? Will you live in the lust of your flesh or with the mind of Christ? Read Romans 8:5–6 and 1 Peter 4:1–2.

Memory Verses

PHILIPPIANS 2:5–8

5 Let this mind be in you, which was also in Christ Jesus:

6 Who, being in the form of God, thought it not robbery to be equal with God:

7 But made himself of no reputation, and took upon him the form of a servant, and was made in the likeness of men:

8 And being found in fashion as a man, he humbled himself, and became obedient unto death, even the death of the cross.

The Committed Mind

Key Verse
PSALM 119:11
11 *Thy word have I hid in mine heart, that I might not sin against thee.*

Lesson Summary
Who doesn't want to be successful? If each person had the choice to live a meaningless life or a life overflowing with success, I guarantee that each one would choose to succeed hands down! Success is coveted, worked for, sought after, and for most, a distant dream. However, success comes from the one source that we have been studying—it's obtainable! According to Joshua 1:8, it comes as a result of "meditating" on God's Word, and we can't meditate on something that we haven't put in our hearts! This lesson concludes this study on the mind by showing the importance of Scripture memory and by giving practical steps on how every person can fruitfully memorize Scripture with a committed mind.

Lesson Aim
To encourage students to implement Scripture memory into their lives.

Introduction

_____

_____

_____

I. The Important _____

A. *Specify a _____ in _____.*

B. *Specify a _____ to _____.*

II. The Inclusive _____

A. *Consider the _____.*

B. *Choose a _____.*
DEUTERONOMY 6:9
9   And thou shalt write them upon the posts of thy house, and on thy gates.

DEUTERONOMY 17:18
18   And it shall be, when he sitteth upon the throne of his kingdom, that he shall write him a copy of this law in a book out of that which is before the priests the Levites.

DEUTERONOMY 27:3, 8
3   And thou shalt write upon them all the words of this law, when thou art passed over, that thou mayest go in unto the land which the LORD thy God giveth

thee, a land that floweth with milk and honey; as the Lord God of thy fathers hath promised thee
8   And thou shalt write upon the stones all the words of this law very plainly.

Front of the card:

Hell #1

Back of the card:

Psalm 9:17

The wicked shall be turned into hell, and all the nations that forget God.

Front of the card:

Hell #2

Back of the card:

Matthew 3:12
Whose fan is in his hand, and he will throughly purge his floor, and gather his wheat into the garner; but he will burn up the chaff with unquenchable fire.

III. The Intent of _____

A. *The reason to be* _____

B. *The reward to the* _____

IV. The Interesting _____

A. *The body's* _____

B. *The body's* _____

V. The Intense _____

A. *The* _____ *to review*

B. *The* _____ *to review*

VI. The Intent _____

A. The _____ of a moment

B. The _____ of memorizing

Conclusion

_____

_____

_____

Study Questions

1. In what verse of the Bible is the word *success* found?

2. The first step to memorizing Scripture is to choose a specific time and a quiet place. This week, write out when and where you can plan to memorize Scripture.

3. The purpose of memorization is to be able to recall Scripture when you need it and for the purpose you need it. Decide today what topic of verses you would like to begin memorizing; list the topic and three verses to correlate with it (i.e., Topic: Prayer. Verses: Psalm 55:17, Mark 1:35, and Hebrews 4:16). Take one step further and write these verses out on 3x5 cards.

4. What did Jesus use in response to Satan's temptation? Refer to Matthew 4:4 and Deuteronomy 8:3.

5. Explain in your own words what the following verses have in common: Luke 11:28, Matthew 7:24, and Revelation 3:22

6. Scripture memory takes both time and work. After hearing these words, many cringe and shy away from starting the process of memorization. If your life is busy already, consider giving up something on your schedule to set aside time to memorize God's Word. What is an area in your life that you can replace with time in God's Word?

7. Read Colossians 3:16. What does God want to richly dwell in us?

8. After learning the importance and practicality of Scripture memory, write out three reasons God would want you to memorize Scripture.

Memory Verse

JOSHUA 1:8

8 This book of the law shall not depart out of thy mouth; but thou shalt meditate therein day and night, that thou mayest observe to do according to all that is written therein: for then thou shalt make thy way prosperous, and then thou shalt have good success.

For additional Christian
growth resources visit
www.strivingtogether.com